Love God

(A True Story)

✓ Alcoholism / Addiction

✓ Anxiety

✓ Depression

✓ Money

✓ Sex / Marriage

✓ Recovery / Faith / Victory

JASON HASLBECK

Table of Contents

Dedication

Love God was written to address the mental/spiritual health crisis that is plaguing our society today. To the millions of people in this world who are struggling with life issues, this book is for you.

Personally, I am dedicating this book to all my friends and family who have passed away from alcoholism, addiction, and suicide. May you rest in peace. Additionally, I am dedicating this book to my father-in-law, Ted Schab, who I am one hundred percent certain is waiting for me in Heaven. We miss you, Dad. I am also dedicating this book to my immediate family including my parents, Jim and Jessie, my mother-in-law Vicki, my twin sister Jenny, my wife Hope, my son Hugh, and the Stall family. Thank you for your unconditional love and encouragement.

Lastly, I am dedicating this book to all my friends and extended family members who have also played an instrumental role in my life – thank you.

Acknowledgments

I would like to first acknowledge The Lord God Almighty. In this mystery of life, there is nothing more important and real to me than Your Holy presence. Thank You, God, for loving me so much.

Also, I would like to thank the following pastors, spiritual advisors, and media outlets for their major impact on my life.

Daystar TV: Marcus and Joni Lamb, Perry Stone, Dr. David Jeremiah, Andrew Womack, Jimmy Evans, Jesse Duplantis, and Joel Osteen.

Son Life Broadcasting Network: Jimmy Swaggart, Francis Swaggart, Donnie Swaggart, Gabriel Swaggart, Loren Larson, and Josh Rosenstern.

Trinity Broadcasting Network

Hillsong TV

K Love Radio Station

Word FM Radio Station

Pastor Tony and Jami Stephens

The Ministry of Gary Yagel

Mark and Adrienne Fiscus

The Holy Bible

You version Bible app

Celebrate Recovery

The Big Book of Alcoholics Anonymous

AA Sponsor Tom Gillespie who led me to Christ

Finally, I want to acknowledge the following outspoken Christian celebrities who have provided me with the additional courage to author this book.

Chris McClarney, Casting Crowns, Mercy Me, Lauren Daigle, Chris Tomlin, Newsboys, For King & Country, Toby Mac, Hillsong United, Big Daddy Weave, David Crowder, Mandisa, Zach Williams, Danny Gokey, Rend Collective, Jeremy Camp, Lecrae, Josh Wilson, Jordan Feliz, Amy Grant, Michael W. Smith, Justin Bieber, Tim Tebow, Kurt Warner, Tony Dungy, Ray Lewis, Steph Curry, Russell Wilson, Manny Pacquiao, Gabby Douglas, Chris Paul, Bubba Watson, Kevin Durant, Carson Wentz, Hulk Hogan, Russell Wilson, Denzel Washington, Kathie Lee Gifford, Stephen Baldwin, Kanye West, Glenn Beck, Mike Lindell, Eminem, and Kirk Cameron.

About the Author

Jason Haslbeck has a knack for writing entertaining and provocative inspirational books. Originally from Baltimore, Jason and his wife, Hope, now live in Pennsylvania with their son, Hugh. For his day job, Jason owns an executive search firm that has been in business since 2009.

His true passion, however, is helping people overcome life issues, afflictions, and relationship challenges. Jason is a deacon in his church, leading a men's recovery and discipleship ministry. Additionally, he is a guest speaker for businesses, churches, and schools across the region.

Lastly, he and his wife are co-founders of Love God, an entirely self-funded Christian ministry that provides humanitarian aid and spiritual encouragement to people in their community.

In his free time, Jason is usually busy coaching his son's sports teams or trying to figure out how to hit a golf ball. After twenty-five years of playing the sport, his game is still in need of a dire miracle.

Introduction

Do you desire personal victory, joy, and true peace of mind? My name is Jason Haslbeck, and I am the author of Love God. This real-life testimony will take you on a roller coaster ride to the gates of hell, and back again. On my kamikaze mission for truth, you will explore the darkest valleys of brokenness and scale the highest mountaintops of freedom - without ever having to leave your couch.

Money, sex, drugs, alcohol, marriage, recovery, and faith will be addressed. There will be no stone unturned. When it comes to personal development books, this one will leave you doing some major soul searching. Through an unfiltered lens of rigorous honesty, readers will be exposed to a biblical worldview that is eye opening and powerful.

OK, who is ready to get this party started? Well then, buckle your seat belts, and put your tray tables up, because we are now cleared for takeoff.

Enjoy the ride!

Running with the Devil

July 24th, 2010

"Hello, my name is Jason, and I am an alcoholic."

"Hello Jason!" said the group of recovering alcoholics sitting in the basement of the musty old church in Baltimore.

It was the twelve-noon meeting that I regularly attended on Fridays to get spiritually tuned up before the weekend. Fridays were always a big trigger for me as I always had a work hard, play hard mentality.

However, this AA meeting was special to me because I was given my first ever 90-day chip for continuous sobriety. It was the longest sobriety run of my 34-year lifespan at the time. When the group asked me to share, I gladly began touting my success. "Today, I celebrate 90-days of continuous sobriety, and I feel like I have been given a new lease on life. I love sobriety! This 12-step program has changed my life, and I am grateful for everyone in this room who has stood by me during this journey so far. Thanks for letting me share, and I will keep coming back!"

My share was short and scripted, but I was still successful in mustering up small applause from the other group members. That meeting was on July 24th, 2010, and I can vividly remember thinking to myself that this sobriety thing was a walk in the park. With a clear head and a prideful

1

spirit, I left that meeting feeling like I was bullet-proof. I thought to myself, "See, I'm not an alcoholic."

It was a beautiful, sunny day, and I could feel the spirit of excitement in the summertime air. Upon leaving the meeting, I was no more than twenty yards outside the church when my eye caught a beautiful woman walking down the street wearing a skimpy sundress. Suddenly, my God-like serenity was replaced with very devious thoughts, and almost immediately, my spirituality evaporated. How the heck did that happen so fast? At the same time, as if the devil had my phone number, I also received a text message from an old drinking buddy who invited me down to Baltimore City to watch the Orioles Game at Pickles Pub (a notorious watering hole right next to Camden Yards Stadium).

Shockingly, it was only sixty seconds earlier that I felt like Pope Francis, and now I was faced with a major temptation. All my previous AA training suggested that I should decline the invitation as hanging out in a bar at 90-days sober was not conducive to maintaining my sobriety. In one last desperate attempt to get my mind back in the right place, I took out the 90-day sobriety coin I had just received five minutes earlier. Unsuccessfully, even the AA coin did not have the power to overcome this seduction, and it only took a nano-second for me to respond to his text message with two words. *Game time!*

The wheels were now in motion and the train immediately left the station. This locomotive was heading downhill and began picking up steam – nothing could stop me now. Of course, I needed to pre-game, so I stopped at the liquor store for a bottle of Captain Morgan and mixed it with a little bit of Coke. It was a toxic blend of booze and caffeine that hit me right between the eyes. I had not partied in over three months, so the dopamine in my brain was firing on all cylinders with anticipation of the night ahead. Plotting out the party, I immediately called my drug dealer and asked him to meet me at the bar with an eight ball of cocaine, which was enough drugs to kill an elephant. The exhilaration I felt on the ride down to Baltimore was intoxicating. By the time I got to the bar, I was feeling like Superman and was ready to party. Supercharged with sin and laser-focused on the party ahead, I was officially off to the races and running with the devil.

Pay to Play

July 26th, 2010

Trying to recollect what happened the previous day and night was difficult, but I do remember a few details that I will summarize to paint a picture of how this party ended.

After 24-hours of binge drinking and drugging, I surprisingly do recall my last drink being a vodka tonic at a very shady gentlemen's club in Baltimore City called, "The Goddess". It was now 4 pm on a Sunday, and I was still up from the night before. The exotic dancers were starting to get sick of me as I had been there all day and was now the only person in the club. These were the first-shift girls, and they were hungry for money. Because I was smashed, they knew they had a big fish on the line and began circling me like sharks. Before I knew it, the club manager notified me that my bar tab had just exceeded $1,500 and it was now time to close out my tab. In a moment of alarm, I suddenly discovered that my wallet and cell phone were stolen by one of the dancing sharks. Out of the corner of my eye, I then noticed the 250-pound bouncer covered in tattoos and face jewelry standing behind the club manager in a show of intimidation. And, regrettably for me, the only credit card I had left was being used to secure the bar tab, and that had just been declined.

At this point, I knew I was in big trouble. Judging by their positioning, they knew I was a flight risk and were plotting how they would dispose of me while still making a profit. I was drunk, high as a kite, and completely out of options. The only two choices left for me were fight or flight. Being an ex-All American college lacrosse player, I knew that I would toast them in a foot race if I could just get out the door. So, I gave them my classic split dodge and blew past them like a bat out of Hell. As I busted through the front door and onto the busy streets of Baltimore, I was immediately blinded by the afternoon sunshine. Loaded up on booze and cocaine, I had a vampire reaction to the light and almost collapsed to the ground. Once I got my bearings, I promptly turned on the jets and went flying down the street weaving in and out of random bystanders. Sure enough, the bouncer was right on my tail and was breathing down my neck like a cyclops from a netherworld. Suddenly, about two hundred feet down the street, I started to realize that my once nimble feet started to feel like 50-pound cinder blocks filled with vodka. It was right at that moment when the bouncer finally caught me and did his best Ray Lewis impersonation by tackling me to the ground. The fight did not last long as he quickly rendered me unconscious with a Green Beret chokehold.

The next thing I remember was waking up in handcuffs in the back of a Baltimore City paddy wagon. I was covered in blood as the bouncer really had his way with me before the cops came. I knew the drill and was on my way to Central Booking, Baltimore City's infamous prison. At this stage in my life, I had been a frequent customer at this Hell hole. The year was 2010, and this prison was one of the worst in the country with multiple humanitarian violations. Subsequently it was forced to shut down a couple years later because so many people were dying while incarcerated. It was a real pleasure palace!

Once transported from the paddy wagon and into Central Booking, the prison had an unmistakable smell of rotten flesh. By this time, my handcuffs had been on my hands (behind my back) for almost three hours as I sat and waited to be booked. To this day, I still have nerve damage in my hands from a lack of blood circulation. Finally un-cuffed, I was put into a 15' x 15' concrete cell with nine other inmates. We were nine maniacs in a box which was a scary piece of real estate. Fortunately, this was not my first rodeo, and I knew my best chance to avoid rape or getting my butt kicked was to keep my head down and not make eye contact with anyone. The most ominous part about being locked up in Central Booking is that you are housed with the worst of the worst (murderers, rapists, gang members, etc.). These people are waiting to be charged and are highly volatile caged animals. Everyone in Central Booking is detoxing from drugs, which exasperates their unfriendly disposition and usually provides a backdrop for physical altercations.

This prison had a 72-hour rule where you legally had to be released before 72-hours or be transferred to the long-term stay portion of the prison. They pushed me right to the limit, and I spent three wonderful days (and nights) in this concrete block with my newfound cellmates. As the only white guy in the cell, I was forced to lay on the concrete floor directly beside an open-air toilet where I witnessed a nine-man excrement bonanza every hour.

When food was served, which was rare, it was moldy and inedible. It did not matter anyway because what food was salvageable was immediately stolen by my roommates. The worst part about being locked up was that nobody on the outside knows where you are. My family and friends thought I was dead for three days as my cell phone was turned off, and I was nowhere to be found. In the movies, you are legally entitled to a phone call, but this luxury hotel must have eliminated that feature to cut down on overhead. Needless to say, my experience in Central Booking in Baltimore City was a living hell, and I still have nightmares to this day.

Baba O'Riley

1989

After a story like that, it is important to briefly look back at my childhood to better understand how I ended up in this jam. First off, I have no excuses. Growing up, I was raised in a middle-class neighborhood in Baltimore by two very loving and supportive parents. Like most childhoods, I remember the long summer days filled with the wonder of being blissfully ignorant about the harsh nature of the real world. As my parents advanced their way out of the middle class, we ended up moving to the county outside of Baltimore and nestled into a great community with a decent public school system.

From a spiritual perspective I was brought up Catholic. However, except for being strong armed by my parents to church on Sundays, and mandatory CCD classes, following Jesus was not a major priority in my life. Actually, He was not even on the radar screen. It was the '90s and I guess you could say that I was your normal run-of-the-mill teenage boy. I played Super Mario Bros (first edition) on the Nintendo, drank water straight from the garden hose, and always was riding my BMX bike.

Now, I don't remember a lot about my childhood, but the one thing I do remember vividly was the first time I drank alcohol. I was fourteen years old at the time, and a bunch of my buddies from the local sports team were on an overnight camping trip. One of the dads was there as the chaperone which was a complete joke. We were all up to no good and he was completely oblivious.

Randomly, I was bunked in a tent with a kid who had smuggled in some peach schnapps from his parent's liquor cabinet. Stored in a mason jar previously filled with jelly, he unscrewed the lid and offered me a sip of the high-octane cocktail. At first, I resisted the offer. But then, he pulled a cassette player out of his duffle bag and put the headphones over my ears. He said, "Listen to this song." It was Baba O'Riley from The Who. You know the song, otherwise known as *Teenage Wasteland*. It only took about 30-seconds of listening to The Who before I lost in my staring contest with the jar of booze. As the devil's music flowed through my ear canals, I took the jar from his hands and fired back a swig. It was such a taboo feeling. I knew that I was doing something wrong. Feeling the burn go down my throat and then the alcohol rushing into my brain was an experience that I will never forget. I felt like a rebel scientist conducting a twisted experiment on my soul. Regrettably, what I did not know at that time was that this harmless experiment was the starting point in creating a real-life Frankenstein.

The Beast

1990 – 1993

Sure enough, after my *Teenage Wasteland* experience, I almost immediately started a devious pattern of seeking alcohol rather frequently. Like most people, alcohol for me became an experimental escape from reality, and I found the feeling of being mentally impaired incredibly enjoyable.

If I am being honest, I knew at a young age that something was missing in my life. I felt insecure about my identity, and I think this was another reason why I turned to the bottle looking for answers. I even remember having thoughts to myself while growing up as a teenager that my reckless behavior was somehow going to kill me one day. I was convinced that there was no way I would live to see the age of twenty-one. And, when I reached my twenty-first birthday, I thought it was a lock that I would be dead by twenty-five. Surprisingly, God had different plans.

On a lighter note, one of the highlights of my teenage years was when my parents bought me my first car, a 1986 Chevy Blazer. This vehicle was equipped with an after-market MTX stereo speaker box that was so loud it rattled your internal organs. I still have "Hells Bells" by AC/DC ringing in my ears thirty-five years later!

With vinyl seats and a rubber floor lining, the car was uniquely qualified to transport drunks. Sadly, drunk driving back in the early '90s was sort of an art form, and I definitely considered myself a Picasso. Notoriously, my 1986 Chevy Blazer quickly obtained the nickname, 'The Beast'. This was mostly because the floor always had a thin layer of dried-up Milwaukee's Best on it. Additionally, my vehicle had a tank-like reputation for running over stop signs, mailboxes, curbs, parked cars, or anything else that got in its way.

And when I wasn't engaging in reckless partying, I was usually found on the lacrosse field. Lacrosse in Baltimore in the '90s was really starting to take off, and my high school lacrosse team was super talented. My senior year team was stacked with all-stars, and we eventually made it to the Maryland State Finals. Even though we ended up losing that game, the after-party was extremely successful in blotting out any sadness from the loss. Win or lose, I was always drinking.

Despite my high school years being loads of fun, the consequences from my irresponsible lifestyle began pouring in (pardon the pun). As you can imagine, I began to experience significant challenges with holding down summer jobs, getting good grades in school, and avoiding Johnny Law. Generously, the cops back in the '90s were very lenient about drinking and driving, and I was very lucky not to get any convictions despite multiple encounters with the police.

By the time I got to my senior year in high school, my college options were limited. With a C+ grade point average and low SAT scores, I was not a real attractive prospect to the Ivy League schools. As luck would have it, I was recruited to play lacrosse at a small Division III liberal arts college in Virginia. When I found out that this school was voted the #1 party school in Playboy Magazine a few years prior, I knew it was my destiny! Adios high school and hello college!

Animal House

1993 – 1997

Because my college did not have a football team, lacrosse was the big sport on campus. Quickly, I became a star as my skills really improved once I graduated high school.

But this stardom went to my head, and I really thought I was something special. Fueled by a steady stream of alcohol, and constant attention for my lacrosse success, I ended up being a drunk egomaniac who never went more than two or three days without being stoned or obliterated. Sure enough, in my sophomore year, I was pressured to leave the school for a semester due to poor grades and a slew of disciplinary measures.

My temporary hiatus landed me at a community college in Baltimore. Yet again, I was the star lacrosse player, and our team made it to the Junior College Championship Game. The only reason we lost the game was due to half the team not going to bed from partying the night before. Lacrosse has certainly come a long way since the '90s!

After being kicked out of college, most normal people would take time to reflect on their behavior and make some changes. However, when I returned to my four-year liberal arts college the following semester, I picked up right where I had left off as if the party never stopped.

13

And, when given the invitation to join a fraternity, I jumped on that train and rode it into the ground. My leadership as Vice President of that fraternity my senior year, or lack thereof, contributed to the eventual closing of the chapter and getting kicked off-campus. Thankfully, however, I saw this crisis as an opportunity and ended up forming a new unofficial fraternity where I did not have to comply with collegiate regulations. My new fraternity was called the OCC, otherwise known as the 'Out of Control Club.' As a founding father, this organization focused strictly on debauchery, insane partying, and self-destruction. Booze, pot, cocaine, acid, mushrooms, pills... it didn't matter. I was a party animal and treated my body like a human garbage can.

During Christmas break that year, while home from college, my parents had me see a doctor because they were concerned about my behavior. When the doctor asked me if I was drinking alcohol or using drugs, I told him that I had a "few beers on the weekends" like all the other kids at college. Little did he know that he was sitting across from Eddie Van Halen on crack! The doctor quickly diagnosed me as having A.D.D. (attention deficit disorder) and gave me a 6-month prescription for Ritalin. I thought this was wonderful, and upon returning to campus, I quickly began crushing and snorting the Ritalin for recreational pleasure. Ritalin became my poor man's cocaine.

Looking back, it is safe to say that my college years were flushed down the drain. It was such a lost opportunity too. My academic and athletic performance were severely handicapped due to my partying and there is no telling how successful I could have been if I was sober.

Even though my college years were one big party, deep down inside those insecure feelings of my childhood were subtly getting worse. Fortunately, the beer kept flowing, and the liquid courage was always there to pick up my spirits. Yes, my college days were a real animal house experience. But, by the grace of God, I eventually graduated with a Bachelor's Degree in Marketing and was now ready to take on the world!

King of Baltimore

1998

After graduating college, most normal people usually put their hard-core partying days behind them and become responsible members of society. On the other hand, I decided to delay my transition into the professional world by backpacking through Europe instead. My little hiatus took approximately two months, and I traveled all the way to Budapest and back again. There was not much sightseeing going on because I was tripping on liquid acid most of the vacation. High-grade liquid acid, coupled with European hash, really turned me into a space cadet who ended up bouncing around from one red-light district to another. I do not know where Europeans get the idea that Americans are obnoxious because I behaved like perfect gentleman!

Upon returning to Baltimore from my European adventure, I was half-baked and finally ready to enter the professional workforce. Despite a below-average GPA in college, my resume did include some accolades that caught the eye of several hiring managers in Baltimore. Remember the college fraternity that I burned to the ground? Well, on paper, it did not look so bad because my resume said I was Vice President of that fraternity. Additionally, I was an Honorable Mention All American lacrosse player, which implied that I had grit and a competitive spirit.

16

Legitimately, a positive attribute that I did offer potential employers was that I was very business-minded and had exceptional communication skills. Some would even say that I was a natural-born salesman. And as luck would have it, fresh off the European acid trip, it only took one interview for me to secure my first job out of college. It was a high-profile job as a Regional Sales Manager for a tractor-trailer staffing company in Baltimore. Astonishingly, for the late '90s, I had the potential to make over six-figures if I hit my sales targets. Not bad for a twenty-two-year-old kid fresh out of college who majored in booze and women's studies!

With this newfound success, I decided to celebrate this windfall by going on an unhinged shopping spree. Neglectfully, I must have skipped the class in college that taught fiscal responsibility and living within my means. Right after my second paycheck, I promptly financed a waterfront row home in Baltimore City close to the Inner Harbor. It was the ultimate bachelor's pad with a rooftop deck and within walking distance to all the bars and clubs. Before the ink was even dry on the mortgage paperwork, I procured a crane company to airlift a 6-person hot tub on my rooftop deck as the cherry on top!

My employer also offered me an auto stipend which I used to buy a new Nissan Maxima, a hot car back in the day. To add to the excitement, without ever having driven a motorcycle previously, I thought it was a great idea to buy a Kawasaki Ninja crotch rocket to shoot around town on the weekends.

Because my job had me overseeing a lot of cash money from processing weekly payroll, I thought it would be appropriate to buy a 9mm handgun to keep with me in my vehicle for safety. Looking back at my twisted and delusional mind, I really thought I was a character from the show Miami Vice.

One night, after smoking a bong hit, and soaking in my hot tub, I remember looking up into the starry night and thinking to myself that the sky was the limit to my success. As a shooting star passed over my head, I felt like I was on top of the world. Yes indeed, the King of Baltimore had taken his throne!

Catch Me If You Can

2000

Skipping ahead, it was the millennium, and I was determined to party like it was 1999. Around this time in my story, I was about twenty-five years old and was extremely active in the dating scene. One evening, on my way to pick up my date of the week, I decided to pregame with a few cocktails and some blow to straighten me out. Instead of the Maxima, I decided to take the Ninja motorcycle as I was really trying hard to make a great first impression with my lady friend.

On a side note, do you remember earlier when I was a teenager and was convinced that I would die before the age of twenty-five? Well, this story might add some relevant color to that premonition. As stated previously, I did not have much experience riding motorcycles and certainly not while intoxicated. And my biggest handicap on the bike was when it came to making S turns at high speeds. And, sure enough, this evening, my questionable ability was put to the test.

There is nothing more exhilarating and powerful than having a rocket attached to your crotch. Motorcycles are a wild ride, and I felt the rush that evening as I was pushing over 100 mph going up the freeway to pick up my date. Out of the corner of my blurry eye, I noticed a cop parked behind

19

an exit sign and then heard the dreaded sound of the siren. Looking in my side-view mirror, my suspicion was confirmed with flashing red and blue lights going off in the distance. As my heartbeat increased tenfold, I intuitively knew I had to make a run for it because I was legally impaired and driving very recklessly. To my demise, the cop must have had a souped-up engine as he quickly gained ground on me. Knowing that I might have been outmatched on the freeway, I made a quick decision to jolt off the exit ramp and proceeded to launch through a four-way stop sign without stopping. Luckily, there was no other traffic at the intersection, or I would have been disintegrated, and this story would be over. However, this tactical risk paid off, and I created some separation between our two vehicles. This side road whined back into the woods, and there was a hairpin turn quickly approaching. Tragically, my S turn skills reared their ugly head, and I ended up wiping out and tumbling upside down into the bushes of a residential property directly off the road.

It was around eight o'clock at night, and I instinctively knew to kill the lights on the bike in hopes that the cop would just fly by without seeing me. And wouldn't you know it, the flashing lights and siren went screaming by without stopping! Horribly for me, the homeowner was home and saw the entire fiasco unfold right in front of his front door.

Storming out of the house, he was initially concerned for my safety. But then he put two and two together and quickly realized that I was a fugitive running from the cops. His words were harsh, and his tone was loud as he yelled, "Stand down," while quickly dialing 911 from his cell phone. Disregarding the homeowner, I clawed my way out of the bushes and began trying to frantically pull my motorcycle out with me. The owner kept screaming at me to stay put, but I did not listen. The bike weighed a ton and was stuck in the mulch. With a herculean effort, I finally got the bike upright and hit the start button. Just my luck, the engine was flooded!

With the homeowner now standing in front of my bike trying to block my escape, I had this sinking feeling that I was busted. Underneath my breath, I said a quick prayer, "God help me." As if an angel touched me, I hit the switch one more time and finally got the engine to light up!

I threw back the throttle, and my bike made a demonic growl. The spinning rear tire created a snowstorm of mulch and dirt that covered the house, and eventually the homeowner, as he dove out of the way. Rocketing up the driveway, I took off in the opposite direction from the cops and could immediately taste freedom on the horizon.

Speeding away, I did a quick inventory to see if any major damage was sustained to me or the bike. Despite a missing fender and some dirt stains on my jeans, my bike and I were miraculously in one piece. However, the adrenalin had me shaking uncontrollably, and my heart was still in my throat. I had a moment of clarity for a quick second and knew that I was completely out of control and should turn myself in to the police. Opportunely, I was able to quickly drown out those thoughts by pulling into a local bar down the road. Hiding my motorcycle behind a dumpster in the parking lot, I bellied up to the bar and ordered a shot of Jack Daniels straight. Once the whiskey ran its course, I left the bar, took a swift detour up the road, and was only 10-minutes tardy in picking up my date. If she only knew!

Downward Spiral

1998 – 2008 (decade of destruction)

When I set out to author this book, my goal was to keep it short and sweet. If we had time, I could share a thousand stories about my crazy lifestyle back in the day. Truthfully, it is not fun for me to reminisce about who I used to be as it is very unsettling. Therefore, I am going to try to condense my life from 1998 to 2008 into one chapter which is appropriately titled, 'Downward Spiral.' So, here it goes...

Per the previous chapters, in my own egocentric mind, I considered myself the King of Baltimore. If you have not noticed, my lifestyle after college was three times crazier than it was when I was in college. What was different from college was that I now had money. And having money opened Pandora's Box to anything and everything a man could ever want if he was willing to cross the line. As you will soon see, not only did I cross the line, but I went over the edge.

I would argue that my lifestyle during my 20's and early 30's resembled a Charlie Sheen interview. My only objective was to make lots of money so I could fuel my non-stop party lifestyle. My moral compass was shattered, and I was hedonistic to the core.

To add to my temptation, Baltimore was littered with bars and nightclubs in neighborhoods like Federal Hill,

Mount Vernon, and Canton. They were only a five-minute drive from my waterfront home, and only a two-minute drive if I was on my motorcycle. This logistical convenience made it super easy to party hard and stay in the fast lane. Additionally, I started noticing advertisements for "Ladies' Night" on Wednesdays at this new bar called the Gin Mill, which was the new hot spot in town. On the weekends, I was successful in pulling off a 24-hour bender without too many consequences. However, Ladies' Night was on a Wednesday night, and that usually did not bode well for my Thursday and Friday work production.

So rapidly, my professional career also started to experience adverse side effects from my partying ways. It was not too long before my employer started noticing a reduction in performance and a consistent pattern of calling out "sick." Apparently, the bartenders at the Gin Mill were over-serving me the night before. And wouldn't you know it, after only being employed for only 12 months, I ended up losing my dream job because of my drinking.

If I was honest with myself, I probably knew that I had a drinking problem. At age 23, however, whatever self-reflective thoughts of morality I had were quickly drowned out by the next happy hour. And because I was a gifted salesperson, I was always able to secure the next six-figure sales job without skipping a beat.

Expensive golf trips, insane bachelor parties, and exotic vacations were a monthly routine. On the weekends, I practically lived at a place called Dewey Beach, which was the party capital of the Delaware Shore. This place was an alcoholic's paradise. The bars opened at 9 a.m. and were packed with young professionals all looking to let their hair down and blow their cash. For me, however, booze was never enough, and I was always trying to extend the party with a bag of ecstasy or cocaine. I am certain that the only people on planet earth who partied harder than I did at Dewey Beach are now six feet under.

At one point in my professional career, I even deviated from white-collar sales and began peddling drugs to supplement my income. Living in an alternative reality, I really thought I was a drug lord who was starring in an X-rated film. Just like the Greek mythological character, Aphrodite, I truly considered myself a 'love god.'

However, on the inside, nobody really knew the true nature of my increasing desperation. Fooling everybody, I was always wearing the nicest suits to work during the week and driving the nicest cars. Maxed out in credit card debt, I quickly became an expert in finding creative ways to finance this never-ending hole in my soul. When my alcohol and drug-fueled bravado wore off, the only thing that remained was my dwindling self-esteem and financial insecurity.

And, sure enough, this perpetual cycle of self-destruction also started having additional legal consequences.

Thinking back to the first chapter of this book, do you recall the story of my strip club adventure with the angry bouncer chasing me down the streets of Baltimore? This might sound shocking, but that arrest was not my first run-in with the law. In fact, my first DWI occurred when I was only nineteen years old. And over my drinking career, my rap sheet included arrests for three DWIs, two drug possession charges, two theft charges (both at strip clubs) and multiple fighting and drunk and disorderly charges. And due to the hefty legal fees, I quickly learned how to beat the system by representing myself in court as my own attorney with a staggering success rate.

Oh, and I almost forgot about the hospitals. It is difficult to remember how many hospitals I visited because of drunken injuries and mental health exams - all of this while wearing a three-piece suit and driving a Porsche 911 Carrera. In the end, I was a sham of a human being and a menace to society. I must have had multiple guardian angels, as it is an absolute miracle that I did not kill myself or someone else during this decade of recklessness. Wait! That statement is not true. If you keep reading this book, you will soon discover that murder could also be added to my scorecard.

See, most alcoholics lead a double life where they hide their secret and insidious behavior from the public eye. In my case, I lived a triple life and was usually aided and abetted by a few unsavory characters. Unfortunately, their names were me, myself, and I.

Drafting this book today and highlighting my destructive and irresponsible past is very disturbing for me. It might seem like I am revering my behavior, but please know that this story has a cataclysmic shift in tone for good. I hope and pray that you will continue reading as I promise this is not where the story ends!

Rehab is for Quitters

2008

Even though I thought I was hiding my maniacal lifestyle from my family and close friends, people started to recognize that Jason was off the rails. Have you ever seen the TV show, *Intervention*? Well, imagine being the recipient of three separate interventions from your family and friends. Just like on TV, they never went well. My interventions were comparable to pulling a wild tiger out of the jungle and telling it to eat only vegetables. Honestly, you could have put the entire National Guard in front of me, and they could not stop me from drinking. In my mind, my entire identity was built around alcohol, and they were trying to strip me of my identity. Alcohol was my god!

However, in January of 2008, when I hit another bottom, my family forced me into a 30-day inpatient rehab facility just outside Baltimore. Upon entering, I really thought I was special because I ended up staying in the same room as the famed comedian, Chris Farley, who later died from an overdose shortly after his stay. Dismally, my level of sickness was no laughing matter, and I finally began to realize the gravity of my situation.

Even though this rehab was $25,000 a month, and served filet mignon and yoga, I was still surrounded by severely broken people. Isolated from reality, we were a tribe of misfits and lost souls. Proudly, it was not too long before all my new rehab friends gave me the very flattering nickname, "Train Wreck." Keep in mind that this was coming from a congregation of crazy people. This certainly should give you some additional insight as to the state of my own mental condition at that time.

Looking back, my rehab experience was one of a kind. It was January 2008, and the rehab was covered in ice and snow. The campus sat high above a frozen reservoir, and there was a chapel located at the end of a bluff that overlooked the water. Every morning, the sun would rise and create this glorious scene where the ice turned into illuminated crystals.

One morning, I decided to go into the chapel and do some genuine soul searching. The sun was reflecting so much light through the church windows that the stained glass looked like it was on fire. It was at that point, all alone in the chapel, that I decided to go back to my Catholic roots and began to pray. Almost immediately, I started sobbing like a baby. Through my tears, I started begging God for forgiveness and asking Him to help me. Even though I had only been clean and sober for about seven days, a flood of peace and serenity poured into my heart that I had never experienced before. To say this was a 'God moment' would be an understatement.

Something big happened in that chapel as I started seeing things at the rehab completely differently. Here is a notable example. A couple of days after my spiritual awakening in the chapel I was attending a rehab education class and an incredibly attractive female in the group slipped me a handwritten note asking me if I wanted to meet her after the class for some inappropriate adult activity. I thought this was a little forward and nerve-racking considering that I just had my 'God moment' a couple of days earlier. And, of all places, the lady suggested the chapel as the target location for this taboo encounter. Normally, I would have left class early and set up a love nest under the altar, but something was different this time. Somehow, I knew that would be terribly wrong. Taking the moral high ground, I took the note and threw it in the trash. In hindsight, I now know that the devil was at that rehab facility, and he was disguised in Spandex!

Yes, a miracle happened in that rehab. After 30 days of inpatient treatment, I came out a changed man. Honestly, I received a world-renowned secular education on the disease of alcoholism, addiction, and mental illness. The most surprising piece of information I learned was the fact that alcohol was a drug in the depressant category. Though legally taxed by our government, alcohol when abused, apparently has some very negative side effects, including

30

impaired judgment, hangovers, ruined relationships, prison, etc. I suppose that's why the beer commercials always said "drink responsibly" at the bottom of their advertisements. Oops, I must have missed the fine print.

Upon graduating from the 30-day inpatient program, the friendly rehab staff even equipped me with a post-rehab action plan that suggested becoming an active member of Alcoholics Anonymous. Returning to Baltimore, after a 30-day disappearance from reality, it was strange to realize that the world kept turning without me at the center of it. I assumed that there would be a big welcome home parade honoring my return from battle. What I quickly realized, though, was that people really did not care that I was gone, and I do not blame them. I was a selfish and irresponsible child who had warped his brain into insanity through extensive use of drugs and alcohol.

Comprehending the true nature of my condition was a humiliating and eye-opening experience. Contrary to my belief that I was the King of Baltimore, I was just another bozo on the bus who was very confused and misguided.

One Last Gasp

2008 – 2010

Despite my taboo encounter with the female patient, the 30-day inpatient rehab program provided me with the most valuable education in my life, up to that point. Yes, even more than my Bong Hits 101 class I took in college. I was now thirty-two years old and had never been continuously sober for this long. It was unchartered territory for me, but I loved my newfound sobriety. In addition to joining AA, my rehab staff told me that I needed to change "people, places, and things."

One of the biggest challenges for someone in recovery is overcoming the enabling influences of friends and family. Even though these people are sometimes great people, and usually come from a place of love, enablers have a negative impact on someone who is trying to get sober. Whether it is providing financial assistance, or minimizing the severity of the behavior, enablers make it harder for an addict to hit bottom. But painful consequences are exactly what is needed to help motivate a person who is battling an addiction to become more responsible in their decision-making.

For me, my first test out of rehab came about five months later when summer arrived, and the biggest party weekend of the year reared its ugly head: Memorial Day. It was the Thursday before Memorial Day weekend, and I had just

32

received a phone call from a long-lost drinking buddy who invited me to come down for the weekend to the beach. Now, let us pause for a moment and think about all the demented stories I have highlighted in the previous chapters of this book. Think about how I spent the previous decade and a half in and out of institutions, locked up in jails, and practically tasting death.

However, none of that mattered. The thoughts of bikinis and beach bars were too overpowering. Once again, and without any recollection of the previous 15 years of alcoholic tragedy, I jumped into my Porsche and zipped through the gears all the way to the shore. This is another clear example of the insanity of alcoholism. Despite all the harmful side effects of alcohol, an addicts brain says it is a promising idea to drink the poison and jump back on the merry-go-round of self-destruction.

On the ride down, my genuine intentions were that I was going to "take it easy" and avoid the hard alcohol (beer only). Upon arriving at the shore house, my friend knew that I had just graduated from rehab and was very hesitant in offering me a beer. However, like the slick salesman I was, I had convinced him that the rehab people said I was allowed to drink. I told him that it was really the drugs that were the problem, not the alcohol.

So, after five months of sobriety, I had my first beer, and I can honestly say I drank it like a polished aristocrat. With obvious hesitation, he offered me a second beer which I also drank very responsibly as we caught up and told old war stories. See, I could drink responsibly!

However, it was not until we left the house and walked into the beach bar packed with bikinis that I had my nuclear meltdown. The music was blaring *Party in the USA* by Miley Cyrus, and it was a half-naked dance party. As one might guess, when the bartender served me that third beer, all hell broke loose. I do not know what was in that third beer, but after five months of sobriety, it tasted like liquid gold. Almost immediately the devil horns began to supernaturally rise out of my forehead, and my eyes turned red. A sleeping giant was awakened, and I was back!

Because we did not have any cocaine, I experienced a legitimate Class "A" blackout that night. And whatever spiritual freedom and serenity I had acquired from rehab completely vanished. After a three-day bender, I returned to Baltimore feeling very defeated and hopeless. Whatever evil spirits I had exorcised during my rehab treatment came back with friends. The scary part about this time was that I had a head full of rehab education and a belly full of booze. Every time I took a drink, I was trying to drown out the truth of what I had just learned, which turned into a psychological nightmare.

There was a major battle going on inside me between good and evil, and it was a very frightening place to be. For the next two years, my life began to unravel even further into the abyss. Adding to the insanity, all my friends and family knew I had been to rehab and thought I was sober, so I now had to begin the charade of hiding my drinking. This only increased my isolation and led me to hang out in the darkest corners of Earth. Even my super shady enabling drinking buddies had disappeared. All I was left with were an onslaught of demons.

After every bender, my hangovers progressively got worse and worse. And the morning after I was usually greeted with shame and remorse for the embarrassing things I did when I was drinking. Hopelessly, the only way I knew how to cope with those negative emotions was to crawl back into the bottle and numb myself with more liquor. Like a dog returning to its own vomit, I was trapped in a vicious cycle of alcoholic madness.

Whatever possessions, money, self-esteem, and relationships that remained were now gone. My drinking and drug use reached an extremely dangerous place where death was imminent. And, due to my extreme selfishness, I left a long trail of tears and broken hearts in my wake.

35

Because I was dead broke, the bank had repossessed my Porsche and had already begun the foreclosure proceedings on my condominium. Basically homeless, I was now living in the condo illegally as a squatter. In the end, all I had to my name was a black leather couch and a flat-screen TV that played the movie *Predator* on repeat non-stop. To this day, I still cannot look at Arnold Schwarzenegger because I will throw up. My downward spiral had reached the end of its rope. I could not imagine living a life without alcohol, but if I kept drinking, I was surely going to die.

OK, let's hit the pause button again. Now I am going to take you full circle in my story one last time. Let us go back to the first chapter of my book where I was tackled outside the strip club and taken away in a paddy wagon. Unbelievably, that strip club and prison experience was when I officially hit rock bottom. It was July 26, 2010, and after being locked up numerous times previously, this was my last and final visit to jail. It was in that cell, curled up in a ball on the concrete floor, where I fully conceded in my heart that I was an alcoholic. Despite the expensive rehabs, and countless interventions, it was in a prison cage where I completely surrendered my will and decided to turn my entire life over to God – all of it.

Even though I was locked up for three days without food, I felt more freedom than ever before. Once I was released from jail, I knew exactly what I needed to do. I re-joined AA and began relentlessly seeking God with all my heart, mind, and soul. I knew that if I followed the directions of AA, and began working the 12-step program, God would take care of me and that is exactly what He did!

Love God

2010 - Present

As I author this book in 2022, it is hard to believe that I have not had a drop of alcohol since that strip club chase back in 2010. Yes, over twelve years of continuous sobriety! Most shockingly, even the mere thought of having a drink makes me disgusted. For a guy who was psychologically and physically addicted to alcohol and drugs for 20-years, how is this even possible?

Well, from a secular perspective, I had to accept the indisputable fact that I was abnormally allergic to alcohol - just like I am allergic to the drug Penicillin. If ingested, both drugs are harmful to me and could have potentially negative side effects. And, because alcohol is a drug, and I had developed a dependency to this drug, I also had to own the label of being a drug addict. Ouch, that hurts!

Unfavorably, this label has a negative stigma and can be confusing as not all alcoholics and drug addicts are the same. For example, some people only drink wine, while others love their beer. Some only drink on the weekends, while others drink every day after a hard day's work. Now that it is legal, many people these days are potheads. And some people like me are binge drinking party animals. The universal commonality, however, is that if your life has become unmanageable (to any degree) due to the use of alcohol, or any other drug, then you should probably stop using drugs. Hmmm, that sounds logical.

But now that I have been sober for a long time, I realize that alcohol and drugs were never my core problem. More than a *drinking* problem, my biggest issue was that I had a *thinking* problem. Addiction psychiatrists believe that alcoholism is a mental illness and a multi-generational hereditary disease. I guess that is true as I was certainly sick in the head.

However, if I am being brutally honest, the root cause of my issues stemmed from a lifelong pattern of misguided and irresponsible decision-making. Additionally, I lacked integrity with other people and was incapable of being honest with myself about my own selfish behavior.

And spiritually speaking, I had a big God-shaped hole in my soul which I tried to fill with anything externally that might provide me with peace. Alcohol, drugs, sex, food, money - but none of it worked. They only provided temporary relief, and I was never completely satisfied, always wanting more, never truly content with life.

When dissecting the program of AA, one of the biggest misconceptions is that it is a stop drinking program when it is actually a start living program. Out of the entire 12-step program, alcohol is mentioned only one time in the first step. All the other eleven steps are about cleaning up the wreckage

39

of your past and re-building your character. Nonetheless, the ultimate purpose of AA is to find God, and that is precisely what happened to me.

By the grace of God, I did not have any felony offenses on my record and was successful in getting all my misdemeanor convictions permanently expunged. It was a humble beginning and there definitely were not any hot tub rave parties anywhere on my social calendar. Finally, at thirty-five years old, I was starting to behave like a responsible adult.

At this stage in my recovery, my primary focus in life was my spiritual development. I was working the 12-step program of AA relentlessly and had already reached the third step where you decide to turn your life (and will) over to God. In overcoming alcoholism, you need to surrender to win. So, I gladly put up the white flag and completely surrendered my life to AA, and to God. This was a huge step, and I made sure I did not gloss over it half-heartedly. Even though I did not really know God, I was told to, "fake it until you make it." And that is exactly what I did in the beginning. But it was not too long afterward when miracles started happening – big time!

One afternoon in September, about three months sober, I was lying on my couch in my newly rented apartment just outside of Baltimore. I will never forget this day. The sun was shining through the sliding glass doors, and there was a gentle breeze coming through the open windows. Although it was ideal napping conditions, I never in a million years expected what was about to happen next. It was on that couch, all alone, where I had nothing short of a miraculous out-of-body experience.

This will be hard to explain, but here it goes. As soon as I fell asleep, I was immediately transported to a heavenly dimension that was filled with a dazzling light that enveloped my entire being. It was a four-dimensional experience sort of like being in virtual reality, but a hundred times more baffling. Physically, it felt like an overpowering sense of 'love' was penetrating every fiber of my body and was pouring out through me from the inside. Then, in the distant clouds, I saw an enormous glowing angelic being that had a brilliant light shining through it and all around it. It then began communicating to me that He was my Creator, and Heavenly Father, and that He loved me. It was a feeling of peace, joy, and love that was too powerful to describe using words. And then suddenly, I woke up. When I came back to reality on my couch, there were only two words remaining in my mind, "Love God."

More than a spiritual awakening, this message from God was immediately tattooed on my heart, and I have never been the same since. For the record, this was not a normal dream or a figment of my imagination. It was an interdimensional experience. Not only did I see God, but I got a glimpse of heaven. From that moment on, the scales were removed from my eyes, and I realized that all my entire adult life I had been searching for answers in all the wrong places. I had traveled halfway around the world, tasting everything, but always ended up feeling unfulfilled and without purpose.

To my wonderful surprise, with the help of God's divine intervention, I had finally cracked the code to the greatest mystery in life. I now knew that it was only God who could satisfy the deepest yearnings of my soul. Breaking through three decades of lies, I was now living in the sunlight of the Spirit of The Lord.

With my newfound holy perspective, I also started experiencing feelings of joy, peace, patience, and self-control that were historically foreign to me. Another analogy to describe this transformation is that I had been living my life previously in black and white, and I was now living in HD. The ultimate description of this spiritual transformation is portrayed in the lyrics of the song by Chris Tomlin, *Amazing Grace*:

Amazing Grace, how sweet the sound that saved a
wretch like me!

I once was lost, but now I'm found. Was blind, but
now I see.

42

'Twas grace that taught my heart to fear, and grace my
fears relieved.

How precious did that grace appear, the hour I first
believed.

My chains are gone; I've been set free. My God, my
Savior, has ransomed me.

And like a flood, His mercy rains. Unending love, amazing
grace.

Jesus Calling

2010 – Present

Despite my God encounter, when evaluating the depths of theology, I was ignorant about understanding the origins of religion. However, all I knew was that both heaven and God were very real, and faith was a beautiful thing. This soft underlying current of purity and righteousness became my guiding light, and it began to produce a harvest of peace in my life.

Then one day, driving home from an AA meeting, I passed by a non-denominational church and felt this unusual curiosity to walk inside the building and check it out. The church was vacant, and the only thing I could see was this giant cross hanging from the rafters. Still, I felt this subliminal force calling me closer and closer to the cross. Eventually, I ended up sitting down in a pew directly in front of the cross, gazing in silence. Inexplicably, a soft, inaudible voice telepathically communicated to me that if I wanted more of this Godly wisdom, then I had to go directly to the source, which was Jesus Christ. A secular person reading this will chalk this experience up to one too many ecstasy binges at the after-hours dance clubs. However, there is no doubt in my mind that the Holy Spirit was directly communicating to me the most critical message in human history - the cross of Christ.

44

Up until this point, my spiritual education only consisted of what I had learned in rehab and in AA. In AA, I was taught to believe in God, but a God of my own understanding. Although it worked at first, this seemed very vague and ambiguous, and I felt compelled to discover the true nature of God. Ultimately, I wanted more knowledge and understanding. And, sure enough, God delivered.

Leaving the church, I knew that I had an old dusty Bible somewhere at home and I immediately began reading it. Because I cheated my way through college, I was never an avid reader and, as such, had a Cliff Notes mentality right from the start. Opening the book was intimidating because of its size and my noteworthy ignorance of scripture. However, once I got through the cobwebs, I started reading the first chapter of the New Testament entitled, *Matthew*. I remember from my Catholic CCD classes as a kid that Matthew was one of the disciples who walked with Jesus for several years, recording His miracles and teachings. When I began reading, I quickly came upon the verse where Jesus said that the greatest commandment from God was to "love the Lord your God with all your heart, mind and soul" (Matthew 22:37).

In my mind, I was immediately blown away! This verse in the Bible was the exact description of what I had experienced in my "Love God" dream only a week prior.

Remember in my dream when God spoke to me and said only two words, "Love God"? At that moment, I had goosebumps go up and down my spine. This was more than a coincidence and I was determined to investigate further. Like a crime scene journalist, I felt this enthralling desire to seek the truth no matter where it took me. Here is the God of the Universe telling me exactly what I need to do to experience His supernatural power through the Word of God (Holy Bible). *Love the Lord your God with all your heart, mind, and soul!*

Grounded in spiritual truths, good and evil became crystal clear to me, and there was no grey area. So, I continued to live a life of rigorous honesty fueled by the Spirit of God, which was Jesus Christ. Yes, now I was officially born again, and Jesus started living through me, providing me with a sense of personal freedom that I never thought was possible.

From this point on, faith became a black or white issue for me. Either God was real, or He was not. Either Jesus was a fraud, and Christianity is the biggest hoax in human history, or Jesus is the Messiah. Therefore, the first-hand testimony recorded in the Bible by His disciples was either an elaborate fabrication, or it was the truth. And so, I came to a life-changing fork in the road that either God is everything, or He is nothing. I had to make my decision.

Writing this book today, I can honestly say that being an alcoholic was the best thing that has happened to me. If I were not an alcoholic, I would never have been introduced to the 12-step program and found God. Additionally, I know very few alcoholics who are capable of quitting drinking permanently, and I am very proud of this accomplishment – thank you, Jesus! Most importantly, I now have the unique opportunity to help other people have victory in their lives who might be struggling with their own set of demons. Lastly, now that I am a Christian, I no longer must wear the blanket label of being an alcoholic or drug addict. Sober, happy, and liberated from the bondage of addiction, I am now a child of God!

In summary, I now have a choice to make every day in deciding how I cope with life. Some people hit the bottle; some hit the pharmacy; I choose to hit my knees! Profoundly, my new life with God has provided invaluable wisdom, eternal security, and irreplaceable peace of mind. Therefore, it is official. My new drug of choice is Jesus Christ with a little bit of caffeine. There is no better feeling than being drunk on the Holy Spirit. It's a lovely cocktail that provides a spiritual blast of miraculous clarity and self-discipline. Yes indeed, I am high on life, and just like McDonald's, I'm lovin' it!

Ultimately, considering that faith in God is completely "FREE," I quickly determined that Jesus was the best deal in town, and I have been whistling a song of supernatural victory ever since.

Satan, Sin & Death

2010 – Present

OK, if you have reached this chapter, I would like you to put the book down and stop reading immediately. Please do not proceed any further until you get a fresh cup of coffee and a highlighter pen. You must have an open mind and really focus to properly understand the information that is going to be shared in this next chapter.

What you will notice is that the tone of this book is going to shift gears from being wildly entertaining to deeply educational. My prayer for you, the reader, is that you will have an unprejudiced mindset and be unbiased to what is discussed. I promise that the content moving forward will be life-changing and powerful - if you have an open mind.

Let's start at a very high level. According to Google, there are currently 2.3 billion practicing Christians worldwide. And, with over 5 billion copies printed, the Holy Bible is the number one selling book of all time. The next closest book in total global sales is the Harry Potter series at 500 million. Here is another fun fact. According to Wikipedia, The Bible is the most accurately transmitted book in world history. No other ancient book has as many accurately copied original manuscripts (there are presently 5,686 original Greek manuscripts of the New Testament in existence today). Based on the numbers alone, I think it is safe to say that Christianity, and the Holy Bible, are topics that deserve a closer look. Rest assured, the information I am about to share with you in this chapter is the most critical guidance ever recorded.

Sitting at my computer today, I have been ingrained with over ten years of comprehensive biblical research, taught by some of the most prolific Christian pastors, educators, and media resources in the world. Please see my acknowledgments section at the front of this book for specific references.

On average, over the past decade, I have invested at least two hours every day into expanding my education into biblical world history. Considering that I was a pothead in college, and have always hated reading, this yearning to learn can only be described as an act of God. However, even after ten years of research, I am still only scratching the surface of understanding the complex depths of my Judeo-Christian heritage.

Just recently, I enrolled in an on-line graduate program to obtain my Master's in Theology but took a pause to draft this book as I believe my testimony needs to be shared with the world quickly. Sadly, I am losing too many friends and family members to the throws of alcoholism, divorce, mental illness, and even suicide, to delay this message of hope any further.

Again, what I am about to present to you in this chapter is based on the teachings of Jesus Christ which were recorded in the Gospels of the Holy Bible. If you do not know, the Gospels are the first four books of the New Testament and are the firsthand recordings of Jesus's three-year ministry on Earth. The word Gospel means "good news," and it refers to the good news of Jesus Christ, the Son of God, who entered our world to save us from the bondage of Satan, sin, and death. Our society has a hundred different labels describing the broken condition of humanity, which can be very confusing. The Bible, however, makes it simple and easy to understand. Sin is the problem and Jesus is the solution!

Let us start at the beginning. Jesus said that He was the Son of God who is the Creator of the Universe. Wow, bold claim! Jesus also said that He is "the way, the truth, and the life and that no one comes to God the Father, except through Him" (John 14:6). According to Jesus, the entire human race was created to glorify God and enjoy His holy presence here on Earth, and in Heaven eternally when we die. Sadly, sin has diverted humanity onto another course which leads to spiritual separation from God. But it is through His loving mercy that God created a rescue plan for the entire human race. He would sacrifice His only Son, Jesus, to atone for all the sins of humankind. Through the cross, Jesus would pay the ultimate price for our sins (both past and present), and thus satisfy the wrath of God.

For those who believe, Jesus's death is our victory, and the only way for humans to be reconciled to God: "For God so loved the world that He gave His only begotten son that whoever believes in Him should not perish but have eternal life" (John 3:16). Jesus is our high priest and our best friend. He is the rock of our salvation. Again, the God of the Universe sacrificed His own son so that we could be in right standing with Him, our Creator. The magnitude of this event in human history, 2,000 years ago, cannot be overstated.

I get it. The statement above sounds very exclusive and might be an obstacle for people who believe that all roads lead to a universal God. However, the most logical question that must be addressed is the following: If there is another way to secure eternal life after death or overcome sin while on Earth, why did God's plan include the crucifixion of His son, Jesus Christ? God would be an insanely cruel deity to torture and kill His own son if there was another way to achieve His spiritual objectives.

The recorded manuscripts of the early church are incredibly unambiguous, and I find it absolutely fascinating to study these scriptures. Remember that during this period of the Roman Empire, if you said you were a Christian, you were likely stoned to death or fed to the lions. Therefore, how did Christianity explode onto the scene in such a dramatic fashion when there was such grave resistance? Why would thousands of people willingly allow themselves to be tortured and killed for the sake of confessing they are followers of Jesus? Well, the most plausible answer is that the events recorded in the Bible are completely true.

As recorded throughout the Bible, Jesus performed hundreds of supernatural miracles, raising people from the dead, making the lame walk, walking on water, giving sight to the blind, etc. These supernatural events were all recorded by eyewitness testimonies and are precisely detailed in the Holy Bible. Even after His crucifixion, Jesus was seen alive for 40 days after his death, just as He had promised. According to these first-hand accounts, over five hundred people witnessed Jesus, after His death, walking around Jerusalem in plain sight (1 Corinthians 15:6).

And, when Jesus was eventually witnessed ascending into Heaven, He promised His followers that they would inherit the mighty power of the Holy Spirit (Acts 2). For those who believe in Jesus, the Holy Spirit provides a heightened sense of peace, wisdom, patience, love, and self-control that we cannot achieve by our own efforts (Galatians 5:22). Most importantly, Jesus also said that when it is our time to die, our bodies would experience a supernatural transformation and join Him in another spiritual dimension, called Heaven (1 Thessalonians 4:17). Wow, that sounds like a sweet deal! And all of this does not cost me anything, except faith?

What is really perplexing is that the Bible says that God's Spirit is everywhere. If you lift a rock, He is there. If you split a piece of wood, He is there too. From the depths of the oceans to the ends of the Universe, God is there (Psalm 139:7-12). When looking at the intricate complexities of human DNA, which is like a mini-computer system in our body; or the invisible electricity that powers the human heart; or the vastness of our Universe which is almost boundless, I think it is safe to say that Our Creator is exponentially more sophisticated than we could ever imagine. Even if you do not believe in God, I think we can all agree that whatever power created our outer space which goes on for a gazillion light years must be endlessly more powerful than the tiny brain of a human being.

Stop and think about this. As you are reading this book right now, you are spinning on Planet Earth at 1,000 miles an hour. Our planet is suspended in outer space, perfectly synchronized so that we are not too close to the sun to get incinerated, and not too far away to be frozen like ice cubes. It is mind-blowing to contemplate the supernatural phenomenon of our existence. Life on Earth is a mathematical design of cosmic power that is more advanced than we can even fathom. To drill home this point even further, scientists who operate the Hubble Space Telescope claim they only understand 5% of our Universe, and 95% is unknown. Yikes, we really are clueless children.

What about UFOs? Many people these days, including our government, believe that there have been very credible testimonies of aircraft from another world defying our laws of physics, gravity, space, and time. If you are one of those people, and you believe that those advanced technologies and powers exist, then how can you dispute that Jesus possibly had similar supernatural powers too? I am only making this point for anyone reading this book who might be open minded to the idea of UFOs, and not open minded to the idea of Jesus. I am not saying that Jesus was an alien, but whatever He was, He was certainly out of this world!

For me, I often take these wonders for granted, trapped inside my head, a slave to this world, unable to appreciate the staggering mystery of God. Considering the astounding miracles of mother nature, human and animal reproduction, oxygen, gravity, photosynthesis, and our infinite Universe, I am convinced that it takes more faith not to believe in God than it does to believe in Him. People are always looking for evidence of God when all they have to do is open their eyes. In my opinion, the theory that our amazing planet, and humanity, are a chance result of a random explosion in space, is a more far-fetched hypothesis than believing Jesus is the Messiah.

Ultimately, the most significant hindrance to faith is that we put God in a box confined to the primitive limitations of our minuscule human brain. If what Jesus says is true, and God is omnipresent (everywhere) and omnipotent (all-powerful), I guess we must suspend our limited human reasoning to make this faith thing work (Psalm 139:7-24).

Yes, that is exactly what is required! But, to do this, we must open our minds and have a sizable chunk of humility entrenched into our souls. Regrettably, for an egomaniac like me, humility was always an elusive character trait. But a wise man once said that God will eventually get your attention, either through humility or humiliation. In my own personal journey of faith, I had to be humiliated to finally surrender my pride.

We, mortals, think we are smarter than we are, and that is where the sin of pride is born. Human arrogance is despised by God and that is why pride is the deadliest sin in the Bible. And sadly, because of our pride, we become fearful of what other people think about us - especially if we say we believe in Jesus. Unfortunately, in a society regulated by Hollywood, following Jesus will not get you a lot of Facebook likes or make you go viral on TikTok. So, if you are trying to win a popularity contest, Christianity is probably not going to be your cup of tea.

The Bible says that the underlying current of ridicule and persecution of Jesus Christ comes from the anti-Christ spirit which operates through all human beings on Earth, including you and me! Yes, according to the Bible, Satan is very real and has been actively trying to deceive humanity, persecute Christ, and dismantle the church from the very beginning.

What motivating force do you think is behind Catholic priests who molest altar boys? Or what evil spirit was the underlying reason for the Crusades during the 11th and 12th centuries? And why are pastors and preachers seen on the news getting in trouble for corruption, infidelity, and theft? Even worse, what demonic spirit causes a person to go into an elementary school with an AR-15 and take out a classroom of children? For me personally, where do you think that voice in my head comes from that tells me it is a good idea to go to the liquor store and self-destruct on alcohol?

The Bible says that Satan is the father of lies and the author of confusion (John 8:44). And, unfortunately, the biggest lie that humans believe is that he does not exist. His subliminal, divisive, and deceptive spirit is always in constant conflict with the truth, which is Jesus Christ. "The god of this age (Satan) has blinded the minds of unbelievers, so that they cannot see the light of the gospel that displays the glory of Jesus Christ, who is the image of God" (2 Corinthians 4:4).

Trust me, I get it, from a secular perspective, these statements from The Bible sound completely ridiculous. However, until you have lived on both sides of the spectrum as I have, there is no better explanation to describe this spiritual battle and my own understanding of these biblical truths. The good news is that Jesus already defeated Satan at the cross of Calvary 2,000 years ago. And now as followers of Jesus, we have spiritual authority over him through our faith in the finished work of the cross. This is why the cross of Christ is so important to understand. If what Jesus says is true, the cross is the only way for humans to have lasting victory over Satan, sin, and death.

As stated previously, I now consider myself blessed with the opportunity to have lived two different lives within one lifetime. For the first 35-years of my life, I lived apart from God, spiritually oblivious. But by the grace of God, the wool over my eyes was removed, and God has entered into my life with supernatural clarity. There is nothing in life that is more powerful and amazing than to have this spiritual metamorphosis of heart, mind, and soul.

Please keep in mind that this supernatural enlightenment goes well beyond human understanding. And, for it to work, we must open our minds, have humility, and believe with childlike faith. Yes, I know this might sound foolish to a prideful spirit, but for those who are willing to have faith, it means priceless freedom and unparalleled spiritual victory in life.

According to famed theologian Oswald Chambers, you cannot think your way through spiritual confusion to make things clear. In intellectual matters, you can think things out, but in spiritual matters, you will only think yourself into more confusion. Again, this is a challenging concept to implement; thus, it takes humility and the elimination of intellectual pride to have success.

Why do you think millionaires and billionaires are often miserable and sometimes commit suicide? The simple reason is that all the money in the world cannot buy this precious gift from God. No amount of intellectual achievement can secure this type of understanding. And no accomplishment in life will ever satisfy the deepest yearnings of the human heart. Only God. And, according to Jesus Christ's teachings in the Bible, there is only one way to God, and that is through Him.

Hope

OK, I know I sounded like a preacher in that previous chapter, but I really needed to get that off my chest. Now, back to my story - where was I? Oh right, I got out of jail, joined AA, and then became a follower of Jesus Christ.

I also continued to work the 12-step program of AA, which included making amends to people I had hurt over my lifetime. Righting my wrongs took a lot of courage and humility, but with God, all things are possible (Matthew 19:26). Surprisingly, most people were very receptive to my apology tour. With a great deal of sincerity and humility, I told people that I was deeply sorry for my selfish and inconsiderate behavior. Regardless of what they may have done to me, this was about me cleaning up my side of the street, and I only focused on what I had done wrong.

Remember the $1,500 bar tab at the strip club that I ran out on? Despite the exotic dancers stealing my credit cards, and the bouncer beating me up, I went back a few days after being released from jail and paid the Strip Club Manager what I owed. His jaw dropped when I gave him the check as he was not accustomed to this type of integrity from his normal patrons. After I apologized for my actions and asked him for forgiveness, I could see the Good Lord softening his heart right in front of my eyes. We almost hugged. It was a beautiful thing.

Clearing out all the resentments and mending the broken relationships in my life was a very liberating experience for me, and it catapulted me into another realm of spiritual growth. "Blessed are the peacemakers, for they shall be called sons of God" (Matthew 5:9).

Picking up on my story again, I was only a few months removed from jail and was now living by myself in a newly rented apartment outside of Baltimore. Per my previous chapter, it was by far the most content and peaceful I had ever been in my entire life. I was so happy to have this personal relationship with God that I did not care about anything else. Life was blissful and pure.

Since I was now a practicing Christian, I suddenly felt a calling to stop dating around and find a special woman who could join me in this walk of faith (Genesis 2:24). It was imperative that this lady shared my Christian values and was supportive of my sobriety. Sure enough, God delivered an angel to me unexpectedly, and her name was Hope! Yes, I cannot make this story up. My newfound soulmate's name was Hope!

Ironically, after communicating on the internet, we figured out that we both vaguely knew each other from the bar scene in Baltimore fifteen years prior. Back then, however, she was a goody-two-shoes and would not have touched me with a ten-foot pole.

Nonetheless, on our first date, I spilled my guts to her and told her about the dark and twisted tale of my life. Sparing her the gory details, I told her about my criminal record, my drug and alcohol addiction, and my playboy lifestyle. But, most importantly, I told her about my coming to Jesus and the radical transformation that was occurring in my life. She was floored by my brutal honesty, and our first date could not have been more magical. Jesus said that the truth will set you free (John 8:31). With all our cards on the table on the first date, our relationship was immediately built on an unshakable foundation of trust.

After only dating for a few weeks, we fell undeniably in love and I proposed to her in five months, and then we married a few months later. As Christians, we made a permanent covenant with God before our family and friends at our wedding. God was, and will always be, at the center of our relationship. "Though one may be overpowered, two can defend themselves. A cord of three strands is not quickly broken" (Ecclesiastes 4:12).

We desired to have children, but sorrowfully, Hope had surgery just three months before we met and her OBGYN said that she would never become a mother. Plus, she was almost 40 years old, so Father Time was also working against us. For me, I was not supposed to have children either for more morbid reasons. Grievously, my darkest sins before I knew Jesus was not the prison time, bankruptcy, or drug overdoses. It was the murderous trail of carnage I left behind with the numerous abortions over my dating career (Jeremiah 1:5).

Writing this on paper stirs the deepest sadness in my heart and mind, even to this day. But, if I had any doubts about the awesome power of God's forgiveness, grace, and mercy, all I have to do is look into the big blue eyes of my son, Hugh. Despite my homicidal track record and Hope's medical issues, God blessed us with a perfectly healthy baby boy who was conceived on our honeymoon. There is no better example of God's unconditional love and forgiveness to those who repent from their sins (Isaiah 55:7).

OK, back to marriage; now, let me be clear; being a family man, and having a successful marriage, can be extremely difficult at times. It requires a tremendous amount of arduous work, patience, and love on both parts. In addition to our human shortcomings, according to the Bible, Satan is also trying to destroy marriages and eliminate the nuclear family (John 10:10). With all this adversity, maintaining a successful marriage is a full-time job. But my Christian faith has provided me with the protection, guidance, and supernatural power to have victory in my marriage too. For this to happen, my wife and I must keep Jesus at the front and center of our relationship.

Without Jesus, I am certain that my marriage would be another statistic. Therefore, yes, I am completely dependent on Jesus, and if that makes me weak, then so be it. Without Jesus, there is no accountability. Marriage was created by God and outlined in the Bible as a permanent union between a man and woman. It is a spiritual act, anointed by God, and has incredible spiritual benefits that far outweigh the challenges.

From my experience, the key to a successful marriage is grace and forgiveness. With God's help, I try to offer my wife as much grace as possible, and vice versa. Grace means undeserving love. God loved the world so much that He gave his only son, Jesus, to be crucified for our sins so that we can have eternal life with Him in Heaven (John 3:16). Now that is grace! For me, being mindful of the death of Jesus is the starting point in developing a forgiving heart. Once again, out of reverence for Jesus, and what He did for us at the cross, my selfish pride is replaced with the spirit of humility and love.

What I have learned over time is that love is not only a feeling but an action. "Love is patient; love is kind; love keeps no record of wrongs" (Corinthians 13:4-8). We both make a committed effort not to harbor any resentments from

64

past wrongs and commit toward Christ-like love for each other. There is no better feeling than to be in harmony with your spouse. Marriage can be amazing when you are married to your best friend while having an intimate physical connection.

In the end, my relationship with Hope is always directly contingent on my spiritual condition. If I am in a good place with Jesus, then I will always be in a good place with my wife. Importantly, we must also constantly remind each other of who the actual enemy is when we get into an argument. Remember, the Bible says that Satan is like a roaring lion with a mission to destroy lives, break up marriages, and ruin families (1 Peter 5:8). We must always remember this spiritual truth. Therefore, our prayer life is so critical in ensuring we have spiritual protection from his evil ways. Even though my marriage is not perfect, marrying Hope was the best decision I ever made, and I am certain it is directly in line with God's will for my life.

Look in the Mirror

2010 – Present

The Big Book of AA says that a business that never takes an inventory of its products and supplies will eventually go broke. In the 12-step recovery program of AA, it is in taking a constant personal inventory that distinguishes the professionals from the amateurs. This has been the most vital component to my own personal development.

Having the humility, honesty, and guts to look into a mirror and do a fearless house cleaning is difficult. This means putting pen to paper and making a list of our personality shortcomings. One straightforward way to accomplish this task is to look back at your life and make a list of all the poor decisions you have made previously. When evaluating those actions, it should not be too difficult to identify glaring character defects. This exercise only works if you do it with an AA sponsor, spiritual advisor, or pastor—someone who is willing to be mercilessly honest.

Because I was a saint and remarkably close to being perfect, my inventory list was short and only included a few minor character flaws. Looking back, I was selfish, dishonest, prideful, impatient, judgmental, fearful, gluttonous, envious, jealous, greedy, impulsive, immature, unfaithful, idolatrous, angry, emotionally insecure, lustful, vain, arrogant, narcissistic, backbiter, and a people pleaser. Wow, maybe I do need a Savior!

However, it is in the confession of these sins where the healing takes place. If we sincerely confess our sins to God, we will always be forgiven. But if we confess our sins to another person, we will become healed (John 1:9). Today, this has become a best practice for me as I have several spiritual advisors in my life who hold me accountable for my personal development goals. I am frequently confessing my sins and asking for prayers for my character restoration. For me, this must be done often to avoid being sucked back into the old way of behaving. When praying, I ask God to take all of me and transform me into the image and likeness of His Son, Jesus Christ. The most sobering thought for me, when faced with a decision on how to behave, is quite simple: What would Jesus do? Obviously, I fall short of that goal, but when I do screw up, I try to quickly repent for my sins and re-dedicate my life to following Jesus.

In full disclosure, my biggest challenge in life is resentment. When I am not trusting God, I can become very irritable and discontent with life events and with other people, especially those closest to me. For instance, it is astonishing how quickly my spiritual bliss can evaporate when my wife decides to leave her clean laundry in the basket and waits three days to put it away. This drives me nuts, and I am certain this world would be such a better place if she would just put away her clothes in a timely fashion. For crying out loud, put away the clothes, Honey!

Wow, see? I just showed you how quickly I can get unraveled. Yeah, yeah, yeah, I get it. Don't sweat the small stuff. Well, I am in the business of perfection, and you are getting in the way of me achieving spiritual greatness!

I jest, of course, but do you see where I am going with this? On a serious note, you can see how my selfishness and lack of patience kicks in and creates disharmony in my soul, and adversity in my relationships. It happens so quickly too. Therefore, staying in a place of love and tolerance toward others is a full-time job for me, and I need God's help every day! One of the most impactful things I ever learned in AA was from the book, *The Twelve and Twelve,* which talks about the spiritual axiom, a principle that suggests that "Whenever I am disturbed, the problem always lies within me." Yes, this takes serious spiritual fortitude. But, looking in the mirror constantly has been instrumental in helping me overcome my shortcomings and have healthy relationships with other people.

Another important benefit of taking a personal inventory is recognizing that just like me, all people are broken, and some are just sicker than others. And this self-awareness of my own brokenness is helping me to have compassion for others who may have harmed me in my past or present day.

For example, back when I was eight years old, my next-door neighbor molested me. He took advantage of my innocence, and it was a very unsettling moment in my life. However, I have zero resentment towards him, as I know he was just a sick dude who was fighting his own set of demons. We are called to hate the sin, not the sinner. We are all sinners and have this evil nature inside of us (sin nature) that sometimes causes us to do sinful things.

Understanding this concept, I have completely forgiven my neighbor (even though he never apologized), and I honestly feel totally at peace about the situation. Yup, that's the power of Christ in me. Forgiveness breaks the chains of bitterness and sets the captive free!

Another important fundamental concept that I learned in AA was putting principles before personalities. One of my biggest prejudices against organized religion and other institutions like Alcoholics Anonymous was the hypocritical behavior of their members. For example, some of the most messed up people I know in this world say that they are "Christians." Equally true, I have been to some AA meetings in my day that resembled more of a witchcraft funeral than an AA meeting. Bottom line, you are going to find all types of crazy people in these institutions, just like in any other institution. And trust me, yours truly is leading the pack sometimes.

Human brokenness is everywhere including in our neighborhoods, corporations, small businesses, and government leaders. However, we must put the principles learned in AA and Christianity ahead of the personalities of the people who are involved. We need to see past the sinfulness of humanity and focus on the spiritual principles outlined in the literature and scriptures for guidance. We cannot judge others and use that prideful stance to venture out into life all alone and live on an island. Unity with fellow believers is imperative to having long-term spiritual success in life. We must surround ourselves with other people who have similar spiritual values and goals in life to have lasting victory over the enemy. Besides, there is nothing richer and more flavorful than sharing fellowship with other believers.

OK, back to my own 12-step character modification story. Overall, the Bible calls this character transformation process, sanctification. As believers, we are slowly and sometimes painfully being transformed into the image of Jesus Christ (Colossians 3:5). Unendingly, this process takes a lifetime. I always use the analogy that my sanctification process looks like the stock ticker for Amazon, where it started low and has gradually been increasing northbound with occasional pullbacks. Many times, I take

70

two steps forward, and one step back, but I am certainly heading in the right direction.

No doubt, my personality needs some improvement, and this character redemption process is something that will continue until I meet my Creator. The good news is that I am making progress, and I give all the glory to God. Through the power of the Holy Spirit, He is empowering me to overcome my shortcomings and to emulate Jesus Christ increasingly more every day.

Bathrobe CEO

2010 - Present

In 2010, I was fresh out of jail, bankrupt, and practically unemployable. And would you believe that only three months later, I would be a successful business owner? Yup, I went from being a gutter drunk to now doing business in all fifty states with the largest corporations in America. Most shockingly, I experienced all this professional freedom while wearing only a bathrobe. Seriously, I started my business from scratch from my home office, stepped on the gas, and have not looked back.

OK, for a Christian guy to be touting his professional success, there must be a reason as this is not Christ-like behavior. What happened to all my humility? I am only sharing this information to glorify God as He gave me the supernatural ability to be successful. Additionally, I hope my testimony will inspire others to achieve greatness through the formidable power of Christ. "I can do all things through Christ who strengthens me" (Philippians 4:13).

However, the biggest mistake for people in recovery, or in life, is thinking that if they would only get their money right everything else would fall into place. The truth is that you need to get right with God first, and then He will begin blessing you with true financial freedom, divorced from greed and idolatry. Putting God first in my life is the key to

72

my success, period. When I say I put God first, I mean that I make my relationship with Jesus Christ my number one priority in life - before my wife, before my son, and before my business affairs. Even before my golf game! Wow, to someone reading this who is not a follower of Jesus, this may seem a little extreme. Let me explain.

The Bible says that anything we put before God is called idolatry (which is a sin). And when we choose to be disobedient to God and live in sin, we then lose out on the spiritual blessings of God which are the fruits of His Spirit (serenity, peace, joy, contentment, etc.).

An important best practice that I learned during my stint in AA was to develop a consistent pattern of daily spiritual discipline. Through a lot of hard work and dedication, I have developed a habit of putting God first every day, no matter what. Every morning I dedicate a good chunk of my time to Bible reading, prayer, and meditation. It is mission-critical for me to start my day off on the right foot with spiritual development as this allows the Holy Spirit to begin guiding my decision-making. Yes, that also means that I must wake up early! Benjamin Franklin said, "Early to bed, early to rise, makes a man healthy, wealthy, and wise."

Daily exercise, and eating healthy, are also critically important to being successful in life. A healthy body equals a healthy mind. People wonder why they are overweight, depressed, and anxious; that is because it requires effort, daily commitment, and sacrifice to achieve sustained results. During the week, I try to fast every night starting at 6 p.m. and do not eat anything else until the next morning. At first, this will cause discomfort, especially if you are accustomed to eating a bowl of ice cream before bed. However, over time, it becomes easier, and soon your energy level and self-confidence will only get better.

I only wish I had the motivation to implement this fast strategy on the weekends, but unfortunately, I turn into a wild pig on Fridays at high noon. All kidding aside, if you want to improve your mental state of mind, or lose weight, go for a three-mile walk around the neighborhood. Do not eat anything after 6 p.m. No excuses and don't quit. Do this every day, and over time you will see major physical and emotional improvement. With God, all things are possible! "Do you not know that your bodies are temples of the Holy Spirit, who is in you, whom you have received from God? You are not your own; you were bought at a price. Therefore, honor God with your bodies" (1 Corinthians 6:19-20).

Undoubtedly, the most important thing I do while I am working throughout my day is listen to upbeat Christian praise music. While I am typing away on my computer, the music in the background subliminally lifts my spirit and keeps me focused on Christ. When I am in the Spirit of Christ, God will supernaturally guide my thoughts which provides an increased level of efficiency, and wise decision making.

I also really enjoy reading the Word of God (The Holy Bible). What is cool with today's technology is that I can also watch powerful sermons on my smartphone, from world-renowned pastors, and never have to leave my home. I am much more of an auditory learner versus a visual learner, and this is super convenient. It is the supernaturally inspired Word of God that gives me the wisdom necessary to make the correct business decisions. It is the Holy Spirit that gives me the energy and focus to work hard and never give up. The Lord is my Shepherd, and that is why I am giving Him all the glory and honor (Psalm 63:3-4).

On the flip side, the pursuit of money and greed is another terrible sin I grapple with occasionally. Fortunately, I no longer measure my success by monetary achievement, as that is just a bunch of numbers. Today, my true measure of success is spiritual freedom from sin. If I am in a good place with Jesus, then everything else will automatically fall into place (Matthew 6:33).

Yet, it was not until I began tithing my income (giving 10% of gross income – before Uncle Sam) that God started blessing me with victory over the sin of greed (Leviticus

27:30). They say you cannot out-give God. Well, that has been my experience, and my family and I are routinely giving more every year to charities, churches, and the poor in our community. If I am being honest, Hope is the one with the charitable heart for helping others. I make the money, and she tells me where to spend it, which is a good thing because I am a spendthrift. In fact, left to my own devices, I would probably be dead broke. That is another reason why God put my beautiful wife into my life.

Again, I am only sharing this information with you to show the radical transformation of my spirit and to give all the glory to the life-changing power of the Lord. The Lord giveth and the Lord taketh away. And, in the end, we cannot take a U-Haul with our personal belongings to the grave. Overcoming the spirit of greed, and the fear of not having enough money, is another key to living a life of true liberty. Also, I know firsthand that no amount of money can buy genuine peace and contentment - only Jesus.

Porno & Prophecy

2010 – Present

Porno & Prophecy? I knew that would get your attention! So, this chapter title seems a bit provocative, but hear me out. If you read the previous chapters in this book, you would know that my life before knowing Jesus was rashly promiscuous. Some of my friends would argue that I even resembled a deranged character from the movie, *Boogie Nights*. Therefore, the sex topic is something that I feel compelled to discuss because of the revolutionary impact Jesus has had on this department for me.

Now that I am a married man, and committed to a monogamous relationship with my wife, it is so important for me to get this right. God created sex not only for procreation but also for enjoyment between a husband and a wife with deep spiritual intimacy. There is nothing more satisfying and peaceful than to have a healthy sexual relationship with your wife that is grounded in integrity and faithfulness.

However, because I am human, I will face temptations towards looking or even desiring other women (Matthew 5:28). But I immediately combat those fiery darts by putting on the armor of God. As soon as I have a lustful thought, I immediately capture that thought and make it obedient to Christ (2 Corinthians 10:5). I pull out the sword of the Spirit

(Word of God) and the usual go-to scripture I begin to recite in my mind is, "Thou shall not covet thy neighbor's wife" (Deuteronomy 5:21). Thankfully, when I am in a good place spiritually, my lustful desires are significantly diminished. In fact, I can totally relate to a priest living a life of celibacy as my relationship with Christ (and the peace that comes with it) ends up being more satisfying than even sex! I can't believe I just said that. Somebody needs to give me a temperature check.

On a more somber note, there is no hiding from God. The Bible says that He is an all-seeing God and knows every action, and even our thoughts too (Proverbs 15:3). Remarkably, He knows all our evil thoughts and desires and still chooses to love us unconditionally. Wow, we are so lucky to have such an amazing Heavenly Father!

But just because I am redeemed by God's grace (due to Jesus's death on the cross), this does not give me the green light to live in sin. Sin may seem enticing on the surface, but it is inherently deceitful and always leads to separation from God and dissension in the soul. King Solomon who was the wealthiest and wisest man on Earth 3,000 years ago said that "the fear of God is the beginning of wisdom" (Proverbs 9:10).

For example, I know that if I choose to watch pornography on my computer, God is watching. I do not know about you, but pornography loses its appeal when you know your Heavenly Father is shaking His head in disgust. Plus, looking at those images will severely scar the human brain and eventually lead to a very unhealthy perspective on women, and sex in general. Watching porn also demeans the person on the screen, a person who was made in God's image, a sister or brother in Christ.

Pornography was a major contributor to my demise before I met Jesus, and it completely warped my brain into a lifestyle of compulsive fornication. By the grace of God, however, I have overcome this affliction and can honestly say that the freedom I experience today from being porn-free is priceless. "Finally, brothers and sisters, whatever is true, whatever is noble, whatever is right, whatever is pure, whatever is lovely, whatever is admirable—if anything is excellent or praiseworthy—think about such things" (Philippians 4:8).

Moving on, sex is a funny topic, and I could write an entire novel on this subject alone. What a curse it is to men these days when women are walking around wearing thong bikinis, or Spandex. Back in the days of Jesus, women were covered head to toe, and men still struggled with lust. Today, women are walking around half-naked which creates an incredible temptation for men young and old. And secular society and advertisers are pressuring women to wear these revealing outfits because sex sells. In an age of equality, men should start wearing thong bikinis, and let us see how that impacts women's perspective on their clothing selection. Just kidding!

Tragically, this sexual temptation has turned into a plague and over 50% of marriages today are ending in divorce. People by the droves are being deceived by Satan into believing that the grass is greener in the other pasture. Infidelity is a lie straight from the gates of Hell, and it is destroying more families and souls than anything else on Earth (John 8:44). This disintegration of the nuclear family is causing a collapse in human morality and is becoming a major contributor to the downfall of our society today.

See, when you remove God from society, morality becomes relative to anyone and everyone. And considering the broken nature of the human condition, this is turning out to be a recipe for disaster. As our society continues to become more un-Godly, is it any surprise that it feels like our world is heading to hell in a handbasket? I am not trying to open a bag of worms here, but according to the Bible (Book of Revelation), we are currently living in the end times and our society will continue to go astray until Jesus returns for the final judgment. From a cultural perspective, this is what the Bible says about our end times. "You should know this, that in the last days there will be very difficult times. People will love only themselves and their money. They will be boastful and proud, scoffing at God, disobedient to their parents, and ungrateful. They will consider nothing sacred. They will be puffed up with pride, and love pleasure rather than God" (2 Timothy 3).

If you have not studied biblical prophecy about end times, it is an eye-opening topic and there is no doubt we are right on track. Just another reason why our relationship with Jesus is so critical.

You're right, end times prophecy is a little too heavy for this book. Let's go back to sex! Yes, marriage can be difficult at times. But nothing good in life is easy. For me, my marital commitment is sealed with the blood of Jesus Christ (John 1:7). I know that sounds weird if you are not a believer, but marital faithfulness requires extreme dedication. The same dedication Jesus made to us on the cross 2,000 years ago is the same commitment I made to my wife on our wedding day.

When it is all said and done, prayer is imperative for me to have victory in all facets of my life. The Bible says to pray incessantly (1 Thessalonians 5:16-18). However, it should not be a burden. We should be so in tune with God that we do not need to ask continually for guidance. For me, when I am *in Christ*, my life supernaturally falls into place, while I enjoy the wonderful side effects of His grace. Who would not like to have peace of mind more frequently? Well, it is available to anyone, free of charge, who is willing to have faith and follow Jesus.

No Fear

2010 – Present

FEAR! You have most likely heard that the acronym for fear is, "False Evidence Appearing Real." Yes, spiritually speaking, fear is an illusion, and it is not real. Fear is a tormenting spirit that has been plaguing human beings since the beginning of time. This evil spirit tricks you into believing something that is 'not' true (James 4:7).

If there was a vote, I am sure fear would be nominated as the most dominating force of negativity in this world today. There is not a single person I know who does not suffer from some level of anxiety - and it seems to be getting worse as our society continues to evolve.

For me personally, I always felt insecure and self-conscious before I became a follower of Jesus. And I think this was another reason why I turned to alcohol so frequently. See, before Jesus, I didn't have a healthy coping mechanism to deal with fear and anxiety, so I decided to self-medicate instead. Unfortunately, however, my fears were still there the next morning, and I now also had a nasty hangover to contend with too.

It is so easy to be fearful these days, isn't it? One of my biggest fears is about the state of our nation and the future of my family once I am gone. My normal go-to scripture to combat this evil thought is, "Trust in the Lord with all your heart, and lean not on your own understanding. In all your ways, acknowledge Him, and He will make your paths straight" (Proverbs 3:5). His ways are higher than my ways and trusting in His sovereignty is such a liberating feeling.

Another quick way to eliminate fear is to put on the helmet of salvation and begin meditating about Heaven and remind myself that this life on Earth is temporary, and very insignificant, especially when looking at it from an eternal perspective (Romans 12:2). As citizens of Heaven, we live in this world but are not of this world. And just as we came into this world naked, we will leave stripped of everything too. We are from dust, and to dust we will return (Ecclesiastes 3:20). The only thing that matters is our relationship with Jesus Christ who has all the power here on Earth, and in the next life to come. He is our Defender and Savior!

Once again, I had to develop the spiritual discipline of capturing my fearful thoughts immediately, recognizing they are not true, and make them obedient to Christ (2 Corinthians 10:5). Another go-to scripture for me in battling fear is, "Perfect love casts out all fear" (1 John 4:18). See, love, and fear cannot coexist. God is love, and Satan is the father of lies and the author of confusion. God did not give us the spirit of fear, but of power, love, and a sound mind (2 Timothy 1:7).

The light of God will always defeat darkness. So, I choose to walk in the light. Again, this takes self-discipline and commitment to prayer, as sometimes my fears can be persistent. However, I remain diligent and over time have eliminated a significant amount of fear in my life. Additionally, I am also always trying to praise God. As stated previously, while I am working at my job, or driving in my car, I am usually listening to contemporary Christian praise music. It is impossible to be fearful if you are worshipping God.

Another challenge in overcoming fear is that I sometimes willingly invite evil and fear into my life. It is so easy these days too. Just hit a button on my smartphone and boom; I am immediately swarmed with fear-provoking articles about all the destruction and chaos in this world. The Bible says, "the eyes of a man are the windows to his soul" (Matthew 6:22-23). In an age where social media and news outlets are being paid for mouse clicks, I am starting to realize that I am being manipulated by politically biased organizations who have greedy motives. I never thought that America would be a land of such blatant media propaganda and censorship. If you are looking for evidence of the deceiving tactics of the anti-Christ spirit, all you have to do is turn on your computer or watch the news. Our media's constant broadcasting of divisive and misleading news stories is a major source of revenue and they feed off fear!

It is amazing how much peace I experience in my life when I do not watch the news. Hmmm, maybe God is trying to tell me something! "Do not conform to the patterns of this world but be transformed by the renewing of your mind" (Romans 12:2). By quieting the noise of this world, and spending alone time with God, we gain incredible peace. Try taking a break from watching the news and invest that time into quiet meditation with the Lord and watch what happens! "Be still and know that I am God" (Psalm 46:10).

One additional remedy to conquering fear is the simplest to do. Just breathe! I usually take three deep breaths through my nose, concentrating on a slow and deliberate exhale through my mouth. While doing this, I am imagining I am breathing in the Holy Spirit. At the end of each exhale, I whisper the name, Jesus. Yes, His name alone has chain-breaking power. Almost immediately this meditative breathing exercise will provide tremendous peace and improved focus. This technique, however, only works when you work it. Continuously, we need to develop the daily, and sometimes hourly, spiritual discipline to utilize these God-given tools.

This point needs to be repeated. It is keeping the cross of Christ as the object of my faith which has the supernatural power to overcome fear. Remember, Jesus defeated Satan, sin, and death at the cross. Conceptualizing the significance of the cross in my mind is what truly activates the Holy Spirit and extinguishes all fear and doubt in my life.

Finally, I believe having faith in God, and trusting that He is sovereign, is the most valuable asset in my life. There is so much freedom in letting go of control. By trusting in the Lord that He is in control of my destiny, and the world's destiny, I am immediately released from all my fears. I do not have to play God anymore. I can sit back, relax, and just enjoy the ride. What a wonderful frame of mind! I am convinced that if everyone implemented these simple best practices, our world would have so much peace and tranquility.

As believers, we are no longer slaves to fear, but children of God and co-heirs with Christ. We are going to inherit the kingdom of heaven when we die, and this alone should put a big smile on everyone's face. If we are true followers of Jesus Christ, fear and doubt should rarely exist. Our lives should be an absolute hymn of praise resulting from perfect and triumphant belief in Jesus's victory at the cross.

My Legacy

2022 – Eternity

When I set out to author this book, my primary objective was quite simple. I wanted to create an entertaining, short story, and use my real-life testimony to glorify the hidden treasure of Jesus Christ.

Remember when God revealed himself to me in my Love God dream? For the record, I have no idea why He chose me as I am certainly not special. My only guess is that in God's omnipotent foreknowledge, He knew that I would be obedient to His will and have the courage to tell my story. In that dream, God gave me His marching orders to tell the world about His unconditional love and grace which is available to anyone.

Looking back on this literary adventure, I can say that this book has caused me to reflect deeply on my life, my inevitable death, and my grand purpose. Today, I am forty-six years old which means that I am officially over the hill and that alone is a very sobering thought.

And when thinking about my mortality, I also begin to think about how often I think of other people who have died before me, and how quickly they are forgotten. This is another essential reason why I wanted to glorify Jesus as He is the most significant person in world history (by a landslide). Most of our civilization was formulated on

Christian values, so it is crucial to stop and recognize the historical magnitude of how Jesus has impacted our planet. When compared to Jesus, it is also really humbling to think about how unimportant I will be once I die.

We only get one shot at life and for this reason my life needs to have a noble purpose. For me, just arriving safely to death with a few million bucks in the bank is pointless and has no impact on my eternal security. And sucking back margaritas all day on the beach gets boring and causes headaches.

Jesus said that we were created for one purpose and that purpose is to tell people the good news of who He is. Jesus is the Savior of the world! God so loved the world that He gave His only son, Jesus Christ, to be a sacrifice for our sins. Through our faith in Him, we will be blessed with the mighty power of the Holy Spirit which will provide us with incredible peace while we are here on Earth. Regardless of our circumstances, we can have tranquility, love, and joy through a personal relationship with Jesus.

Miraculously, the only requirement for this blessing is faith. Jesus tells us to love the Lord our God with all our hearts, our minds, and our souls. Secondly, we are to love our neighbor equally as much as ourselves (Luke 10:27). These biblical truths will be the only thing that will matter in the end.

So, the trillion-dollar question is whether Jesus Christ is God, or an elaborate scam? I am convinced that the answer to this question is the principal ingredient to properly understanding this mystery called life. My prayer is that you will investigate this enigma with unparalleled determination and seek the truth no matter where it takes you. You may have to put your Netflix subscription on pause for a few months as this investigation will require some time and effort. The good news is that you will surely know when you find the truth because it will immediately set you free, and you will know peace.

If you have not seen the movie, *The Matrix*, I would highly recommend watching the movie for a couple of reasons. First, it is an excellent film. Secondly, the movie illustrates an excellent analogy of Christianity. It starts with the character Morpheus (played by Laurence Fishburne) offering Keanu Reeves the option of taking either the red or blue pill. If you take the blue pill, the story ends, and you go back to your old life that is hollow, mundane, and controlled by carnal pleasures. However, if you take the red pill (Jesus), your eyes will be opened to the true nature of your condition, breaking the chains that enslave you to this superficial world. Just like Morpheus, Jesus is only offering the truth.

In conclusion, my experience in seeking this truth has opened my mind to a world of supernatural wonder and joyful hope. What I have learned is that God's love for us is beyond our comprehension and all He wants from us in return is our faith. There is nothing we can do to earn salvation, except have a personal relationship with Jesus Christ. And because of this supernatural miracle, believers stand justified, not because we are sorry for our sins, but because of what Jesus has done for us at the cross. The salvation that comes from God is not based on human logic, but on the sacrificial death of His Son. In our obedience to God, we become blessed with an abundant life of peace that is beyond measure and price.

For thousands of generations, since the beginning of time, God has been our eternal rock. And every good and perfect gift in life comes from God. Always remember that God is for us, and not against us (Romans 8:31). So, what are you waiting for? It is time to get on the winning team! For me, I will continue to love God with all my heart and sing His praises where they will echo into eternity forever and ever. Amen!

John 3:16

For God so loved the world that He gave His only begotten son, that whoever believes in Him will not perish but will have eternal life.

P.S.

If you are interested in securing immortality with God in heaven, and experiencing Godly blessings while on Earth, please recite the following prayer.

Heavenly Father, thank You for sacrificing Your Son Jesus Christ on my behalf, to pay the incredible price for the sins I have committed against You. According to Your unfailing love, please forgive my sins and send Your Holy Spirit to be with me now and forever. Jesus, I accept You as my Lord and Savior. Thank you for saving me. Amen!

If you just said this simple prayer, the Spirit of God has now been awakened in your heart. For a next step, I would encourage you to immediately join a vibrant church in your area with conservative biblical values. Don't just go on Sundays but become an active member.

I hope that you have been enlightened and entertained by reading this book. Please share it with others who might need encouragement and spiritual guidance. If you have a minute, thank you for leaving me an Amazon book review. You can also follow me on Facebook by going to my website below. Lastly, if you would like a FREE "Love God" bumper sticker, please just send me a message. God is good!

www.jasonhaslbeck.com

Golden Scriptures

If you read your Bible with holy expectation, meditating on the life-changing words of God, the Holy Spirit will begin transforming your mind and give you an enlightened perspective on life that is worth its weight in gold.

Listed below are my favorite scriptures in the Bible. Memorizing and reciting these scriptures throughout my day gives me incredible joy, wisdom, and peace. If you begin implementing these scriptures into your prayer life, I am very certain you will begin experiencing the same results.

Philippians 4:13

I can do all things through Christ who strengthens me.

Proverbs 3:5

Trust in the Lord with all your heart and lean not on your own understanding; in all your ways acknowledge Him, and He will make your paths straight.

Romans 12:2

Do not be conformed to the pattern of this world but be transformed by the renewing of your mind. Then you will be able to test and approve what is the perfect will of God.

Mark 12:30

And you shall love the Lord your God with all your heart, and with all your mind, and with all your soul. This is the first and greatest Commandment. And the second is to love your neighbor as yourself.

John 15:5

Jesus said, I am the vine; you are the branches. If you remain in me, and I in you, you will bear much fruit; apart from me you can do nothing.

Matthew 6:33

Seek first the kingdom of God, and all His righteousness, and all these things shall be added unto you.

Corinthians 6:19

Our bodies are a temple for the Holy Spirit. Therefore, in view of God's mercy, offer yourselves as a living sacrifice, holy and pleasing to God, which is our spiritual act of worship.

Psalm 37:4

Delight yourself in the Lord, and He will give you the desires of your heart.

Romans 12:1

For God did not give us the spirit of timidity or fear, but of power, love, and self-discipline.

Ephesians 6:12

For our struggle is not against flesh and blood, but against the rulers, against the authorities, against the powers of this dark world and against the spiritual forces of evil in the heavenly realms.

Psalm 23

The Lord is my shepherd; I shall not want. He makes me lie down in green pastures; He leads me beside still waters. He restores my soul; He leads me in paths of righteousness for His name's sake. Even though I walk through the valley of the shadow of death, I will fear no evil; for You are with me; Your rod and Your staff, they comfort me. You prepare a table before me in the presence of my enemies; you anoint my head with oil; my cup runs over. Surely goodness and mercy shall follow me all the days of my life; and I will dwell in the house of the Lord Forever.

End Notes

1. Alcoholics Anonymous World Services, Inc. *Alcoholics Anonymous, Fourth Edition.* Thirty-first printing, 2013

2. Alcoholics Anonymous World Services, Inc. *Twelve Steps and Twelve Traditions Trade Edition*

3. Zondervan Publishing, *Life in the Spirit Study Bible, New International Version.*

4. Jimmy Swaggart Ministries, *The Expositor's Study Bible.* Jimmy Swaggart Ministries Publishing,

5. The Ministry of Gary Yagel. *www.fordgingbonds.org*

6. Oswald Chambers, *My Utmost for His Highest by Oswald Chambers, daily devotional.* *www.utmost.org*

7. *Family Photograph on website by Christina Shea www.jasonhaslbeck.com*

Ingram Content Group UK Ltd.
Milton Keynes UK
UKHW050405200623
423718UK00004B/107